'Know the Game' Series

CRICKET

CONTENTS

(minor amendments incorporated for 1968 season)

Printed in England by John S. Speight Ltd., Yeadon, Yorkshire

FOREWORD

It can be said of most outdoor games that comparatively few of those who play or watch have a really sound knowledge of the Laws that govern them: indeed many players and spectators who are critical of the decisions of umpires and referees might themselves fail dismally to pass an examination in the Laws governing the conduct of the game in question.

This book has been produced for the M.C.C. in the hope that it will encourage cricketers of all ages to make a closer study of the Laws of the game. It is expected that it will thereby lead to a general improvement in the standard of umpiring, particularly at schools. A detailed index is included from which it should be possible to trace the answers to most problems which arise during play.

The M.C.C. have always been prepared to answer questions on the Laws of Cricket on certain conditions which will be readily understood, *i.e.*(*a*) In the case of League or Competition Cricket the enquiry must come from the Committee responsible for organising the league or competition. In other cases enquiries should be initiated by a representative officer of a Club or of an Umpires' Association on behalf of his Committee or by a master in charge of school cricket. (*b*) The incident on which a ruling is required must not be merely invented for disputation but must have actually occurred in play. (*c*) The enquiry must not be connected in any way with a bet or wager.

It should be noted that, from time to time, the M.C.C. try out experimental amendments to the laws in first-class cricket, to see if they are suitable for incorporation into the official Laws at a later date.

Umpires and players are strongly recommended to supply themselves with a copy of the official Laws which can be obtained from most sports firms and direct from the M.C.C., price 1s. net, or 1s. 3d. post free for a single copy.

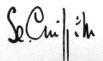

Secretary, **Marylebone Cricket Club.**

THE GAME OF CRICKET

Cricket is an essentially English ball game which has certainly been played from the 16th century, though its origin is obscured by the mists of time.

It is played between two teams, normally eleven a side, and gives the maximum opportunity for combining team effort with individual skill and initiative. Each team bats, or takes its innings, in turn—the choice for first innings being decided by toss. The game is played on a pitch on which two wickets are placed 22 yards apart, though this distance may be reduced for young boys.

The two batsmen defend these wickets against the bowling of the fielding side, and when a batsman is "Out" his place is taken by another, and so on until ten batsmen are out or until the innings has been declared closed.

A bowler from the fielding side bowls an over of 6 balls (8 balls in Australia and New Zealand) from one end at the opposite batsman defending his wicket, and aims to dismiss the batsman in one of the ways provided for in the Laws. The more common methods of dismissing a batsman are the bowling down of the striker's wicket, catching him from a stroke, his being Leg Before Wicket, stumping by the wicket-keeper when he has gone out of his ground, and the running out of either batsman while attempting a run.

Overs are bowled successively from alternate ends. No bowler can bowl two overs in succession, but with that restriction the captain of the fielding side can change his bowling as he thinks fit.

The score is reckoned by "Runs"—that is the number of times the batsmen run from end to end of the area between the "popping crease" at each end of the pitch. Runs are usually the result of hits, but can be scored when the ball has not actually been hit by the striker, *e.g.*, "Byes" and "Leg Byes" or, as penalties for "Wides" and "No Balls" as defined in the Laws.

The fielding side will dispose themselves with the two-fold object of dismissing the opposing batsmen and of preventing them from scoring runs.

When the first side has completed its innings, the other side take theirs. A match may consist of one or two innings by each side, the former being confined to the case of a one-day or half-day game. The side scoring the largest aggregate of runs in the match is the winner. If the match is not played out to a finish it is regarded as drawn. The detailed conduct of the game is governed by the Laws of Cricket with which this book is concerned. We know that the Laws were "settled" or revised in 1744, but long before that cricket was being played under a commonly accepted code. During the heyday of the famous Hambledon Club in the period 1750 to 1790 the Laws gradually developed, but it was not until the formation of the Marylebone

Cricket Club in 1787 that the Laws came under a single central authority.

The M.C.C. has always been accepted as the constitutional authority for revising and giving decisions on the Laws, and the code has gradually developed to meet the changing requirements of the game. Major revisions were carried out in 1835, 1844 and 1947.

Each year the M.C.C. receive from all over the world a stream of enquiries on points connected with the conduct of the game. By far the greater number of these can be answered by a simple reference to a Law, or to an Official Note, but occasionally one may lead to the introduction of a new ruling and sometimes even to a change in the fundamental Laws.

Changes in the conduct of the game necessitate consultation with governing bodies of cricket all over the world, and are never approved until they have been tried out experimentally over several seasons.

The Law and Official Notes, corrected for 1965, are given in full in this book, supplemented with sketches and additional comments based on a review of the more common enquiries which have been received at Lord's since the Code was adopted in 1947. While not being official in the strictest sense, it is believed that these comments represent the best opinion available on points which give rise to uncertainty in the minds of inexperienced players, umpires and scorers.

The term 'Special Regulations' referred to in certain Laws are those authorised by M.C.C., Overseas Governing Bodies or other Cricket Authorities in respect of matches played under their jurisdiction.

SIDES

LAW I. A match is played between two sides of eleven players each, unless otherwise agreed. Each side shall play under a captain who, before the toss for innings, shall nominate his players who may not thereafter be changed without the consent of the opposing captain.

OFFICIAL NOTES

1. If a captain is not available at any time, a deputy must act for him to deal promptly with points arising from this and other Laws.

2. No match in which more than eleven players a side take part can be regarded as First-class, and in any case no side should field with more than eleven players.

KEY

1. Third man	13. Short extra cover
2. Deep fine leg	14. Silly mid-off
3. Long leg	15. Forward short leg or silly mid-on
4. Backward point	
5. Second slip	16. Extra cover
6. First slip	17. Mid-off
7. Short fine leg or leg slip	18. Bowler
8. Square leg	19. Mid-on
9. Umpires	20. Mid-wicket
10. Gully	21. Long-off
11. Wicket Keeper	22. Long-on
12. Cover point	

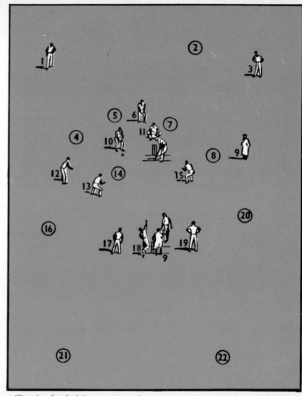

Typical field setting for a medium-pace schoolboy bowler. Figures in circles indicate positions which may be used in alternative field settings.

SUBSTITUTES

LAW 2. A substitute shall be allowed to field or run between the wickets for any player who may, during the match, be incapacitated from illness or injury, but not for any other reason without the consent of the opposing captain; no substitute shall be allowed to bat or to bowl. Consent as to the person to act as substitute in the field shall be obtained from the opposing captain, who may indicate positions in which the substitute shall not field.

OFFICIAL NOTES

1. A player may bat, bowl or field even though a substitute has acted for him previously.

2. An injured batsman may be "Out" should his runner infringe Laws 36, 40 or 41. As *Striker* he remains himself subject to the Laws; should he be out of his ground for any purpose he may be "Out" under Laws 41 and 42 at the wicket-keeper's end, irrespective of the position of the other batsman or the substitute when the wicket is put down. When *not the striker* the injured batsman is out of the game and stands where he does not interfere with the play.

Additional Comments on Law 2.

Notice particularly that a substitute can only be claimed as a right for a player who becomes unfit during the match. In all other cases the consent of the opposing captain is necessary.

Note 1 is important—it means that a player on the team list (Law 1) can bat, even if a substitute has fielded for him throughout an innings. Note also that the Law does not prevent a substitute from keeping wicket.

Regarding Note 2, it is sometimes not appreciated that if the runner is standing in front of the popping crease when the striker is receiving a ball, and the wicket is put down, the striker is out "Run out" although he has never left his ground.

If the injured batsman, when not the striker, brings himself into the game in any way then he must suffer the penalties that any transgression of the Laws demands.

THE APPOINTMENT OF UMPIRES

LAW 3. Before the toss for innings, two umpires shall be appointed; one for each end to control the game as required by the Laws with absolute impartiality. No umpire shall be changed during a match without the consent of both captains.

OFFICIAL NOTE

1. The umpires should report themselves to the executive of the ground 30 minutes before the start of each day's play.

THE SCORERS

LAW 4. All runs scored shall be recorded by scorers appointed for the purpose; the scorers shall accept and acknowledge all instructions and signals given to them by the umpires.

OFFICIAL NOTE

1. The umpires should wait until a signal has been answered by a scorer before allowing the game to proceed. Mutual consultation between the scorers and the umpires to clear up doubtful points is at all times permissible.

Additional Comments on Law 4.

Although the scorers cannot dictate to the umpires they are entitled to question them on any point about which doubt exists. Particularly in practice games played by juniors, they may also call the attention of the umpires to such points as persistent miscounting of the number of balls in the "Over," but play should not normally be interrupted for this purpose. (See also Notes on page 44.)

THE BALL

LAW 5. The ball shall weigh not less than 5½ ounces, nor more than 5¾ ounces. It shall measure not less than 8¹³⁄₁₆ inches, nor more than 9 inches in circumference. Subject to agreement to the contrary either captain may demand a new ball at the start of each innings. In the event of a ball being lost or becoming unfit for play, the umpires shall allow another ball to be taken into use. They shall inform the batsmen whenever a ball is to be changed.

OFFICIAL NOTES

1. All cricket balls used in first-class matches should be approved before the start of a match by the umpires and captains.
2. Except in the United Kingdom, or if local regulations provide otherwise, after 200 runs have been made off a ball in first-class matches, the captain of the fielding side may demand a new one. In first-class matches in the United Kingdom the fielding side may demand a new ball after 85 (6-ball) overs have been bowled with the old one. In other grades of cricket these regulations will not apply unless agreed before the toss for innings.
   Australia 55-65 overs (8-ball). \
   Other countries 75-85 (6-ball). } Experiment.
3. Any ball substituted for one lost or becoming unfit for play should have had similar wear or use as that of the one discarded.

Additional Comments on Law 5.

The provision of a new ball under Note 2 is intended only for the best class of club cricket. It is not intended to apply to one-day cricket, or should the additional expense be an embarrassment.

A small ball weighing 4¾ oz. should be used by young boys. The Women's Cricket Association standard ball weighs 5 oz. and is slightly smaller than the standard size.

THE BAT

LAW 6. The bat shall not exceed 4¼ inches in the widest part; it shall not be more than 38 inches in length.

Additional Comments on Law 6.

The weight of the bat is not specified but a full-sized bat weighs about 2 lb. 3 oz. A boy's batting may be seriously handicapped by use of too large or too heavy a bat.

THE PITCH

LAW 7. The pitch is deemed to be the area of ground between the bowling creases, 5 feet in width on either side of the line joining the centre of the wickets. Before the toss for innings, the executive of the ground shall be responsible for the selection and preparation of the pitch; thereafter the umpires shall control its use and maintenance. The pitch shall not be changed during a match unless it becomes unfit for play, and then only with the consent of both captains.

Additional Comments on Law 7.

The width of the pitch (10 feet) is intended for turf. The width of an artificial pitch is that of the playing surface.

THE WICKETS

LAW 8. The wickets shall be pitched opposite and parallel to each other at a distance of 22 yards from stump to stump. Each wicket shall be 9 inches in width and consist of three stumps with two bails upon the top. The stumps shall be of equal and of sufficient size to prevent the ball from passing through, with their tops 28 inches above the ground. The bails shall be each $4\frac{3}{8}$ inches in length, and, when in position on the top of the stumps, shall not project more than $\frac{1}{2}$ inch above them.

OFFICIAL NOTES

1. Except for the bail grooves the tops of the stumps shall be dome-shaped.
2. In a high wind the captains may agree, with the approval of the umpires, to dispense with the use of bails (see Law 31, Note 3).

Additional Comment on Law 8.

A pitch 21 or 20 yards long is preferable for small boys.

THE BOWLING AND POPPING CREASES

LAW 9. The bowling crease shall be in line with the stumps; 8 feet 8 inches in length; the stumps in the centre; with a return crease at each end at right-angles behind the wicket. The popping crease shall be marked 4 feet in front of and parallel with the bowling crease. Both the return and popping creases shall be deemed unlimited in length.

OFFICIAL NOTE

1. The distance of the popping crease from the wicket is measured from a line running through the centre of the stumps to the inside edge of the crease.

Additional Comment on Law 9.

To be within his ground a batsman must have some part of his bat or person grounded inside the popping crease. (See Law 32)

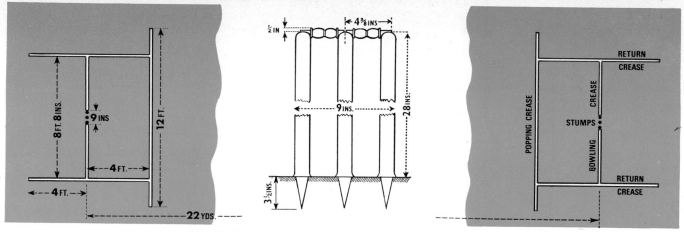

The Pitch, etc.—diagram to illustrate Laws 7, 8 and 9

Experiment:- *Starting in 1967 for all grades of cricket to help the interpretation of experimental law 26 (page 20) the crease markings are now as shown above.*

ROLLING, MOWING, AND WATERING THE PITCH

LAW 10. Unless permitted by special regulations, the pitch shall not be rolled during a match except before the start of each innings and of each day's play, when, if the captain of the batting side so elects, it may be swept and rolled for not more than seven minutes. In a match of less than three days' duration, the pitch shall not be mown during the match unless 'Special Regulations' so provide. In a match of three or more days' duration, the pitch shall be mown under the supervision of the umpires before play begins on alternate days after the start of a match, but should the pitch not be so mown on any day on account of play not taking place, it shall be mown on the first day on which the match is resumed and thereafter on alternate days. (For the purpose of this Law a rest day counts as a day). Under no circumstances shall the pitch be watered during a match.

1. The umpires are responsible that any rolling permitted by this Law and carried out at the request of the captain of the batting side, is in accordance with the regulations laid down and that it is completed so as to allow play to start at the stipulated time. The normal rolling before the start of each day's play shall take place not earlier than half an hour before the start of play, but the captain of the batting side may delay such rolling until 10 minutes before the start of play should he so desire.

2. The time allowed for rolling shall be taken out of the normal playing time if a captain declare an innings closed either (a) before play starts on any day so late that the other captain is prevented from exercising his option in regard to rolling under this Law, or (b) during the luncheon interval later than 15 minutes after the start of such interval.

3. Except in the United Kingdom, if at any time a rain-affected pitch is damaged by play thereon, it shall be swept and rolled for a period of not more than 10 consecutive minutes at any time between the close of play on the day on which it was damaged and the next resumption of play, provided that:

   (i) The umpires shall instruct the groundsman to sweep and roll the pitch only after they have agreed that damage caused to it as a result of play after rain has fallen warrants such rolling additional to that provided for in Law 10.

   (ii) Such rolling shall in all cases be done under the personal supervision of both umpires and shall take place at such time and with such roller as the groundsman shall consider best calculated to repair the damage to the pitch.

   (iii) Not more than one such additional rolling shall be permitted as a result of rain on any particular day.

   (iv) The rolling provided for in Law 10 to take place before the start of play, shall not be permitted on any day on which the rolling herein provided for takes place within 2 hours of the time appointed for commencement of play on that day.

COVERING THE PITCH

LAW 11. The pitch shall not be completely covered during a match unless special regulations so provide; covers used to protect the bowlers' run-up shall not extend to a greater distance than $3\frac{1}{2}$ feet in front of the popping creases.

OFFICIAL NOTE

1. It is usual under this Law to protect the bowlers' run-up, before and during a match, both at night and, when necessary, during the day. The covers should be removed early each morning, if fine.

Additional Comments on Law 11.
Covers are seldom used except in Test, County and other leading cricket. In England complete covering of the pitch is usually restricted to a period of 24 hours before the start and each night of a Test match, and to week-end covering in county matches.

The covers used for the bowlers' run-up are usually about 18 ft. long of which $7\frac{1}{2}$ ft. only projects on to the pitch over the bowling creases at each side.

MAINTENANCE OF THE PITCH

LAW 12. The batsman may beat the pitch with his bat, and players may secure their footholds by the use of sawdust, provided Law 46 be not thereby contravened. In wet weather the umpires shall see that the holes made by the bowlers and batsmen are cleaned out and dried whenever necessary to facilitate play.

INNINGS

LAW 13. Each side has two innings, taken alternately, except in the case provided for in Law 14. The choice of innings shall be decided by tossing on the field of play.

OFFICIAL NOTES

1. The captains should toss for innings not later than 15 minutes before the time agreed upon for play to start. The winner of the toss may not alter his decision to bat or field once it has been notified to the opposing captain.

2. This Law also governs a one-day match in which play continues after the completion of the first innings of both sides. (*See also* Law 22.)

Additional Comments on Law 13.

In half-day cricket, it is often agreed to fix a maximum period for an innings. This is best done by limiting an innings to a stated number of "Overs". (See Law 18.) Note 1 is very important: The toss can take place at any time, but the winner can delay his decision to bat or field until 15 minutes before play is due to start.

FOLLOWING INNINGS

LAW 14. The side which bats first and leads by 150 runs in a match of three days or more, by 100 runs in a two-day match, or by 75 runs in a one-day match, shall have the option of requiring the other side to follow their innings.

Experiment:- In recent years, in matches of more than 3 days, the follow-on has been altered experimentally to 200 runs.

DECLARATIONS

LAW 15. The captain of the batting side may declare an innings closed at any time during a match irrespective of its duration.

OFFICIAL NOTE

1. A Captain may forfeit his second innings. In this event, the interval between innings shall be 10 minutes and his decision must be notified to the opposing Captain and Umpires in sufficient time to allow seven minutes rolling of the pitch.

LAW 16. When the start of play is delayed by weather, Law 14 shall apply in accordance with the number of days' play remaining from the actual start of the match.

START AND CLOSE OF PLAY AND INTERVALS

LAW 17. The umpires shall allow such intervals as have been agreed upon for meals, 10 minutes between each innings and not more than 2 minutes for each fresh batsman to come in. At the start of each innings and of each day's play and at the end of any interval the umpire at the bowler's end shall call "Play", when the side refusing to play shall lose the match. After "Play" has been called no trial ball shall be allowed to any player, and when one of the batsmen is out, the use of the bat shall not be allowed to any player until the next batsman shall come in.

OFFICIAL NOTES

1. The umpires shall not award a match under this Law unless (i) "Play" has been called in such a manner that both sides can clearly understand that play is to start, (ii) an appeal has been made, and (iii) they are satisfied that a side will not, or cannot, continue play.

2. It is an essential duty of the captains to ensure that the "in-going" batsman passes the "out-coming" one before the latter leaves the field of play. This is all the more important in view of the responsibility resting on the umpires for deciding whether or not the delay of the individual amounts to a refusal of the batting side to continue play.

3. The interval for luncheon should not exceed 45 minutes unless otherwise agreed (but see Law 10, Note 3). In the event of the last wicket falling within 2 minutes of the time arranged for luncheon or tea, the game shall be resumed at the usual hour, no allowance being made for the 10 minutes between the innings.

4. Bowling practice *on the pitch* is forbidden at any time during the game.

Additional Comments on Law 17.

Notes 1 and 2 require emphasis. The penalty for "refusing to play" is against the culprit's whole side and not only himself. Any penalty under this Law must be a matter for the joint decision of both umpires. It is the clear duty of the players to avoid creating the circumstances in which such a decision may be necessary.

The 2 minutes allowed for a fresh batsman to go out is more than ample, if the players are alert.

LAW 18. The umpires shall call "Time" and at the same time remove the bails from both wickets, on the cessation of play before any arranged interval, at the end of each day's play, and at the conclusion of the match. An "Over" shall always be started if "Time" has not been reached, and shall be completed unless a batsman is "Out" or "Retires" within 2 minutes of the completion of any period of play, but the "Over" in progress at the close of play on the final day of a match shall be completed at the request of either captain even if a wicket fall after "Time" has been reached.

OFFICIAL NOTES

1. If, during the completion of the last over of any period of play, the players have occasion to leave the field, the umpires shall call "time". In the case of the last over of the match, there shall be no resumption of play and the match shall be at an end.

2. The last over before an interval or the close of play shall be started, provided the umpire standing at square leg, after walking at his normal pace, has arrived at his position behind the stumps at the bowler's end before time has been reached.

Additional Comments on Law 18.

The completion of the last over on the "final day" includes of course the over in progress at the close of play on one-day or half-day matches. For this reason it has been recommended under Law 13 that if definite time for an innings is to be agreed upon, it should be arranged on the basis of an equal number of overs.

Under this Law, provided the first ball of the last over is bowled before time, as many as five wickets might fall after time: indeed the over and the match might not terminate until 10 minutes after time.

SCORING

LAW 19. The score shall be reckoned by runs. A run is scored: (i) So often as the batsmen after a hit, or at any time while the ball is in play, shall have crossed and made good their ground from end to end; but if either batsman run a short run, the umpire shall call and signal "One short" and that run shall not be scored. The striker being caught, no run shall be scored; a batsman being run out, that run which was being attempted shall not be scored.
(ii) For penalties under Laws 21, 27, 29, 44 and boundary allowances under Law 20.

OFFICIAL NOTES

1. If, while the ball is in play, the batsmen have crossed in running, neither returns to the wicket he has left except in the case of a boundary hit, or a boundary from extras, or under Laws 30 (Note 1) and 46 (Note 4) (vii). This rule applies even should a short run have been called, or should no run be reckoned as in the case of a catch.

2. A run is "short" if either, or both, batsmen fail to make good their ground in turning for a further run.
   Although such a "short" run shortens the succeeding one, the latter, if completed, counts. Similarly, a batsman taking stance in front of his popping crease may run from that point without penalty. The above provision will apply if a batsman is "out" off, or "retires" after, the last ball of an over when less than 2 minutes remain for play at the conclusion of the match.

3. (i) One run only is deducted if both batsmen are short in one and the same run.
   (ii) Only if three or more runs are attempted can more than one run be "short" and then, subject to (i) above, all runs so called shall be disallowed.
   (iii) If either or both batsmen deliberately run short, the umpire is justified in calling "Dead Ball" and disallowing any runs attempted or scored as soon as he sees that the fielding side have no chance of dismissing either batsman under the Laws.

4. An umpire signals "short" runs when the ball becomes "dead" by bending his arm upwards to touch the shoulder with the tips of his fingers. If there has been more than one "short" run the umpire must instruct the scorers as to the number of runs disallowed. (See Note 1 to Law 4.)

Additional Comments on Law 19.

In spite of the fact that no runs can be scored if the striker is out "Caught," the non-striker remains at the end he has reached if any runs have been attempted. (See Note 1 to this Law.) In the case of a "Run out" all completed runs count to the batsmen, except that in which the "Run out" occurred, which of course is not a "completed" run.

Particular attention is called to Note 3, in regard to the failure of both batsmen to make good their ground in one and the same run.

BOUNDARIES

LAW 20. Before the toss for innings the umpires shall agree with both sides on the boundaries for play, and on the allowances to be made for them. An umpire shall call or signal "Boundary" whenever, in his opinion, a ball in play hits, crosses or is carried over the boundary. The runs completed at the instant the ball reaches the boundary shall count only should they exceed the allowance, but if the "Boundary" result from an overthrow or from the wilful act of a fieldsman, any runs already made and the allowance shall be added to the score.

OFFICIAL NOTES

1. If flags or posts are used to mark a boundary, the real or imaginary line joining such points shall be regarded as the boundary, which should be marked by a white line if possible.

2. In deciding on the allowances to be made for boundaries the umpires will be guided by the prevailing custom of the ground.

3. It is a "Boundary" if the ball touches any boundary line or if a fieldsman with ball in hand, grounds any part of his person on or over that line. A fieldsman, however, standing within the playing area may lean against or touch a boundary fence in fielding a ball (see *also* Law 35, Note 5).

4. An obstacle, or person, within the playing area is not regarded as a boundary unless so arranged by the umpires. The umpire is not a boundary, but sight screens within the playing area shall be so regarded.

5. The customary allowance for a boundary is 4 runs, but it is usual to allow 6 runs for all hits pitching over and clear of the boundary line or fence (even though the ball has been previously touched by a fieldsman). It is not usual to allow 6 runs when a ball hits a sight screen full pitch, if the latter is on or inside the boundary.

6. In the case of a boundary resulting from either an overthrow or the wilful act of a fieldsman, the run in progress counts provided that the batsmen have crossed at the instant of the throw or act.

7. The umpire signals "Boundary" by waving an arm from side to side, or a boundary "6" by raising both arms above the head.

Additional Comments on Law 20.

It should be noted that if the ball is stopped by any of the obstructions mentioned in Note 4, it remains in play, and a batsman can still be "run out."

The fixing of boundaries usually follows the custom of the ground, and the allowances mentioned in Note 5 are now commonly accepted.

The first part of Note 3 refers to a usual ground on which the boundary is a line and not a fence; the special provision given in the last sentence of the Note applies to the latter.

There is nothing in the Law or Notes to say that a fieldsman must stop a ball from passing over a boundary, but he may not procure that event by a deliberate act, *e.g.*, by kicking the ball, in order to gain any advantage such as preventing the batsmen crossing.

Signal—"Boundary 4"   *Signal—"Boundary 6"*

LOST BALL.

LAW 21. If a ball in play cannot be found or recovered, any fieldsman may call "Lost Ball," when 6 runs shall be added to the score; but if more than 6 have been run before "Lost Ball" be called, as many runs as have been run shall be scored.

Additional Comments on Law 21.

The introduction of boundaries, and the improvement of outfields have rendered this Law almost redundant. It should be noted, however, that the term "lost" is used in the sense of temporarily irrecoverable, which can occur when, for example, the ball is lodged on or in an obstruction in the playing area, or has been appropriated by a dog.

It is, of course, perfectly permissible for a fieldsman to call "Lost Ball" well in advance of the batsmen completing 6 runs in order to restrict the liability to that number, but once called, the ball is "dead" and the penalty is final.

The match ends

THE RESULT

LAW 22. A match is won by the side which shall have scored a total of runs in excess of that scored by the opposing side in its two completed innings; one-day matches, unless thus played out, shall be decided by the first innings. A match may also be determined by being given up as lost by one of the sides, or in the case governed by Law 17. A match not determined in any of these ways shall count as a "Draw."

OFFICIAL NOTES

1. It is the responsibility of the captains to satisfy themselves on the correctness of the scores on the conclusion of play.
2. Neither side can be compelled to continue after a match is finished; a one-day match shall not be regarded as finished on the result of the first innings if the umpires consider there is a prospect of carrying the game to a further issue in the time remaining.
3. The result of a finished match is stated as a win by runs, except in the case of a win by the side batting last, when it is by the number of wickets still then to fall. In a one-day match which is not played out on the second innings, this rule applies to the position at the time when a result on the first innings was reached.
4. A "Draw" is regarded as a "Tie" when the scores are equal at the conclusion of play but only if the match has been played out. If the scores of the completed first innings of a one-day match are equal, it is a "Tie," but only if the match has not been played out to a further conclusion.

Additional Comments on Law 22.

Disputes over the results of matches due to scoring mistakes being discovered too late to correct, are far too frequent. They should not occur if the instructions given in Law 4 and in the notes for scorers and umpires on page 44 are followed.

If the umpires are satisfied that a mistake in scoring has occurred, they may, provided time has not been reached, order play to be resumed, or they may award the match against the side which by its acquiescence in the assumed result has "given up."

In one-day cricket the umpires should always require the players to attempt a two-innings conclusion if there is the least chance of this. It is, however, no part of the umpires' duties to suggest to the captains that any arrangement for dividing the remaining time, etc., should be made.

As soon as a side has won, the match is finished and nothing that happens afterwards can technically be regarded as part of the play. If the scores are even when, for example, the side batting last has lost 7 wickets and a batsman is run out attempting a second run, or a batsman is "out" off a no ball, the correct result is that the batting side has won by 3 wickets as in one case the first run counts, and in the second the penalty for a no ball is not cancelled.

A "Tie" cannot occur in an uncompleted match, *e.g.*, Side A, 1st innings 100, 2nd 200, Side B, 1st innings 200, 2nd 100 for 5, does not represent a completed match and the result is *not* a "Tie."

THE OVER

LAW 23. The ball shall be bowled from each wicket alternately in overs of either 8 or 6 balls according to the agreed conditions of play. When the agreed number have been bowled and it has become clear to the umpire at the bowler's wicket that both sides have ceased to regard the ball as in play, the umpire shall call "Over" in a distinct manner before leaving the wicket. Neither a "No Ball" nor a "Wide Ball" shall be reckoned as one of the "Over."

OFFICIAL NOTE

1. In the United Kingdom the "Over" shall be 6 balls, unless an agreement to the contrary has been made.

Additional Comments on Law 23.

In Australia the over consists of 8 balls. If an umpire miscounts the number of balls, any additional balls are valid.

"Over"

LAW 24. A bowler shall finish an "Over" in progress unless he be incapacitated or be suspended for unfair play. He shall be allowed to change ends as often as desired, provided only that he shall not bowl two "Overs" consecutively in one innings. A bowler may require the batsman at the wicket from which he is bowling to stand on whichever side of it he may direct.

Additional Comments on Law 24.

The umpire should call "Dead Ball" should a bowler be incapacitated while running up to deliver the first ball of an over. The final clause of Law 25 does not apply in these special circumstances, and another bowler should be deputed to bowl an over from the same end.

If, however, one or more balls, even though they be "Wides" or "No Balls" have been delivered before the bowler is incapacitated, a fresh over must be started from the other end.

If an over is left incomplete for some reason at the start of any interval of play, it is finished on the resumption of play.

LAW 25. The ball shall be held to be "Dead" on being, in the opinion of the umpire, finally settled in the hands of the wicket-keeper or of the bowler; or on reaching or pitching over the boundary; or, whether played or not, on lodging in the dress of either a batsman or umpire; or on the call of "Over" or "Time" by the umpire; or on a batsman being out from any cause; or on any penalty being awarded under Laws 21 or 44. The umpire shall call "Dead Ball" should he decide to intervene under Law 46 in a case of unfair play or in the event of a serious injury to a player; or should he require to suspend play prior to the striker receiving a delivery. The ball shall cease to be "Dead" on the bowler starting his run or bowling action.

OFFICIAL NOTES

1. Whether the ball is "finally settled" is a question of fact for the umpire alone to decide.
2. An umpire is justified in suspending play prior to the striker receiving a delivery in any of the following circumstances:
   (i) If satisfied that, for an *adequate* reason, the striker is not ready to receive the ball, and makes no attempt to play it.
   (ii) If the bowler drops the ball accidentally before delivery, or if the ball does not leave his hand for any reason.
   (iii) If one or both bails fall from the striker's wicket before he receives the delivery.

   In such cases the ball is regarded as "Dead" from the time it last came into play.
3. A ball does not become "Dead" when it strikes an umpire (unless it lodges in his dress), when the wicket is broken or struck down (unless a batsman is out thereby), or when an unsuccessful appeal is made.
4. For the purpose of this and other Laws, the term "dress" includes the equipment and clothing of players and umpires as normally worn.

Additional Comments on Law 25.

Umpires should not regard the ball as "finally settled" and therefore "Dead" if either batsman is "out of his ground," of if there is any reason to think it may be to the advantage of the fielding side for the ball to remain in play.

Ball ceases to be "Dead"—see Law 25.

Under Note 3, the ball does not become "Dead" if the wicket is broken either by the bowler during his delivery, or by a batsman in running.

If an umpire is knocked out, his colleague should regard him as a player for purposes of Law 25 and suspend play by calling "Dead Ball."

NO BALL

LAW 26. **For a delivery to be fair the ball must be bowled, not thrown or jerked; if either umpire be not entirely satisfied of the absolute fairness of delivery in this respect, he shall call and signal "No Ball" instantly upon delivery. The umpire at the bowler's wicket shall call and signal "No Ball" if he is not satisfied that at the instant of delivery the bowler has at least some part of one foot behind the bowling crease and within the return crease, and not touching or grounded over either crease.**

OFFICIAL NOTES

1. Subject to the provisions of the Law being complied with a bowler is not debarred from delivering the ball with both feet behind the bowling crease.

2. The striker is entitled to know whether the bowler intends to bowl over or round the wicket, overarm or underarm, right or left handed. An umpire may regard any failure to notify a change in the mode of delivery as "unfair", if so, he should call "No Ball."

3. It is a "No Ball" if the bowler before delivering a ball, throws it at the striker's wicket even in an attempt to run him out (see Law 46, Note 4 (vii)).

4. If a bowler break the near wicket with any part of his person during the delivery, such act in itself does not constitute "No Ball."

5. The umpire signals "No Ball" by extending one arm horizontally.

6. An umpire should revoke the call "No Ball" if the ball does not leave the bowler's hand for any reason.

Experiment:- *Since 1967 for all grades of cricket, a ball shall be deemed to have been thrown if in the opinion of either Umpire the process of straightening the bowling arm, whether it be partial or complete, takes place during that part of the delivery swing which directly precedes the ball leaving the hand. (A bowler can still use the wrist in the delivery swing.)*

Experiment:- *Since 1967 for all grades of cricket it is a "No Ball" if in the delivery stride,*

(a) the Bowler's front foot lands clear beyond the popping crease or

(b) the bowler's back foot does not land completely within the return crease, or its forward extension.

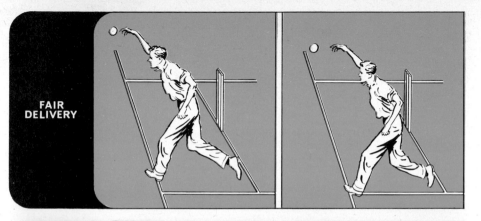

FAIR DELIVERY

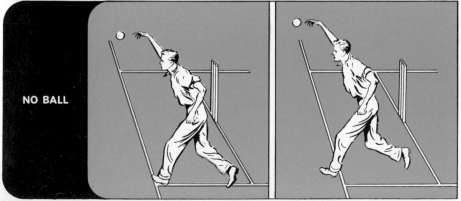

NO BALL

Signal—"No Ball"

Page Twenty-one

LAW 27. The Ball does not become "Dead" on the call of "No Ball." The striker may hit a "No Ball," and whatever runs result shall be added to his score, but runs made otherwise from a "No Ball" shall be scored "No Balls," and if no runs be made one run shall be so scored. The striker shall be out from a "No Ball" if he breaks Law 37, and either batsman may be run out, or given out, if he breaks Laws 36 or 40.

OFFICIAL NOTES

1. The penalty for a "No Ball" is only scored if no runs result otherwise.

2. Law 46, Note 4 (vii) covers attempts to run before the ball is delivered, but should the non-striker unfairly leave his ground too soon, the fielding side may run out the batsman at the bowler's end by any recognised method. If the bowler throws at the near wicket, the umpire does not call "No Ball," though any runs resulting are so scored. The throw does not count in the "Over."

Additional Comments on Law 27.

If the batsmen do not run for a "No Ball" the penalty of one run is credited under extras. If, however, the ball goes to the boundary, or the batsmen run, the actual number of completed runs are entered, but *not* the penalty in addition. If the striker has not played the "No Ball" with his bat, such runs are credited under Extras; if he has touched it, they are credited to his score.

It should be noted that if a batsman is out off a "No Ball"

this does not cancel it, and the penalty or runs completed are still credited to the score.

Note 2 does not require the bowler to warn a batsman at his end who is taking an unfair advantage by backing up before the ball has been delivered, though by convention such a warning is usually given. The bowler can run him out either by putting the wicket down with ball in hand, or by throwing it down.

WIDE BALL

LAW 28. If the bowler shall bowl the ball so high over or so wide of the wicket that, in the opinion of the umpire, it passes out of reach of the striker and would not have been within his reach when taking guard in the normal position, the umpire shall call and signal "Wide Ball" as soon as it shall have passed the striker.

OFFICIAL NOTES

1. If a ball which the umpire considers to have been delivered comes to rest in front of the striker "Wide" should not be called, and no runs should be added to the score unless they result from the striker hitting the ball which he has a right to do without interference by the fielding side. Should the fielding side interfere, the umpire is justified in replacing the ball where it came to rest and ordering the fieldsmen to resume the places they occupied in the field before the ball was delivered.

2. The umpire signals "Wide" by extending both arms horizontally.

3. An umpire should revoke the call if the striker hits a ball which has been called "Wide".

Additional Comments on Law 28.

The use of the word "and" in line 4 of the Law indicates that there are two conditions which must both be satisfied for a ball to be a "Wide"; the first is that the striker is not within reach of the ball even though he may have moved towards it; the second is that the striker cannot create a "Wide" by moving away from it towards square leg.

A "No Ball" by definition is not a properly delivered ball and cannot therefore be a "Wide" in addition.

It should be noted that "Wides" can never be credited to the striker's score since if the ball is struck, the call of "Wide" should be revoked. (See Law 28, Note 3.)

The fact that a batsman may be given out off a "Wide" does not affect the penalty for bowling it, so that the penalty or any runs actually completed while the ball remains in play are credited to the batting side.

LAW 29. The ball does not become "Dead" on the call of "Wide Ball." All runs that are run from a "Wide Ball" shall be scored "Wide Balls," or if no runs be made one run shall be so scored. The striker may be out from a "Wide Ball" if he breaks Laws 38 or 42, and either batsman may be run out, or given out, if he breaks Laws 36 or 40.

Additional Comment on Law 29.

As in the case of a "No Ball," if a "Wide" goes to the boundary or the batsmen run, the actual boundary allowance or number of completed runs is entered as "Wides" under Extras.

Signal—"Wide"

BYE AND LEG BYE

LAW 30. If the ball, not having been called "Wide" or "No Ball" pass the striker without touching his bat or person, and any runs be obtained, the umpire shall call or signal "Bye"; but if the ball touch any part of the striker's dress or person except his hand holding the bat, and any run be obtained, the umpire shall call or signal "Leg Bye"; such runs to be scored "Byes" and "Leg Byes" respectively.

OFFICIAL NOTES

1. The Umpire shall regard the deliberate deflection of the ball by any part of the striker's person, except the hand holding the bat, as unfair, and as soon as he is satisfied that the fielding side have no chance of dismissing either batsman as an immediate result of such action, he shall, without delay, call "dead ball". In deciding whether such deflection is deliberate, the criterion shall be whether or not the batsman has attempted to play the ball with his bat.

Experiment:- *In First Class cricket in the U.K. leg byes will be allowed if the batsman is trying to avoid being hit by the ball when he deflects it.*

2. The umpire signals "Bye" by raising an open hand above the head, and "Leg Bye" by touching a raised knee with the hand.

Additional Comment on Law 30.

Although the word "immediate" is used in Note 1 it is not meant that "Dead Ball" shall be called so quickly as to preclude the possibility of the fielding side dismissing the batsman under the appropriate laws. When the umpire is satisfied that the fielding side have no chance of dismissing either batsman as an immediate result of the batsman deliberately deflecting the ball, he should then call "Dead Ball." The word "immediate" is used to avoid any waste of time involved in the batsmen taking runs which would subsequently be disallowed.

Signal—"Bye"

Signal—"Leg Bye"

"Leg Bye"

THE WICKET IS DOWN

LAW 31. The wicket shall be held to be "Down" if either the ball or the striker's bat or person completely removes either bail from the top of the stumps, or, if both bails be off, strikes a stump out of the ground. Any player may use his hand or arm to put the wicket down or, even should the bails be previously off, may pull up a stump, provided always that the ball is held in the hand or hands so used.

OFFICIAL NOTES

1. A wicket is not "down" merely on account of the disturbance of a bail, but it is "down" if a bail, in falling from the wicket, lodges between two of the stumps.
2. If one bail is off, it is sufficient for the purpose of this Law to dislodge the remaining one in any of the ways stated, or to strike any of the three stumps out of the ground.
3. If owing to the strength of the wind, the captains have agreed to dispense with the use of bails (see Law 8, Note 2), the decision as to when a wicket is "down" is one for the umpires to decide on the facts before them. In such circumstances the wicket would be held to be "down" even though a stump has not been struck out of the ground.
4. If the wicket is broken while the ball is in play, it is not the umpire's duty to remake the wicket until the ball has become "dead." A fieldsman, however, may remake the wicket in such circumstances.
5. For the purpose of this and other Laws, the term "person" includes a player's dress as defined in Law 25, Note 4.

Additional Comments on Law 31.

Particular attention is called to Note 2. The fact that one bail is already off in no way prevents the wicket being legitimately broken by the removal of the other bail.

Regarding Note 4. It will be understood from the Law that even if the bails are off, the wicket can be bowled or thrown down if the ball strikes a stump entirely out of its hole in the ground. Alternatively a player can put down the wicket by pulling up a stump with the hand or hands holding the ball. If all the stumps are on the ground, the fielding side is allowed by Note 4 to put back one or more stumps in order to have an opportunity of breaking the wicket.

Under Law 25, Note 2, if either or both bails are blown off the striker's wicket before he receives delivery, that ball is considered cancelled, but in general the captains should agree under Law 8, Note 2, to dispense with the use of bails if the conditions are such as to make the blowing off of bails likely.

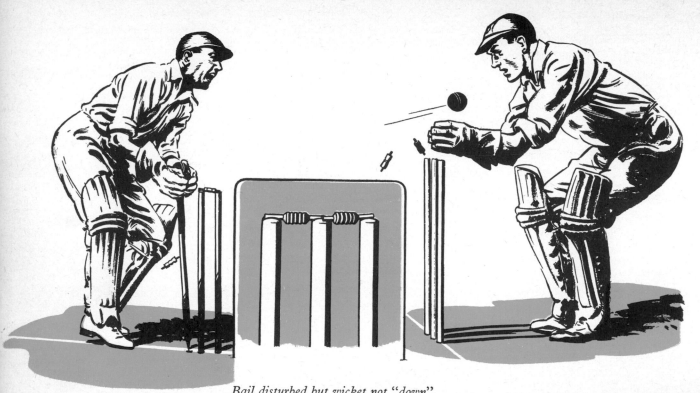

"Out"

Bail disturbed but wicket not "down"
—see Law 31, Note 1

"Not Out"

(above) "*Out*"—*see Law* 31

(at left) "*Not Out*"—*see Law* 31

OUT OF HIS GROUND

LAW 32. A batsman shall be held to be "Out of his ground" unless some part of his bat in hand or of his person be grounded behind the line of the popping crease.

Out of his crease

Bat over but not grounded

"Out"

BATSMAN RETIRING

LAW 33. A batsman may retire at any time, but may not resume his innings without the consent of the opposing captain, and then only on the fall of a wicket.

OFFICIAL NOTE

1. When a batsman has retired owing to illness, injury, or some other unavoidable cause, his innings is recorded as "Retired, Not out," but otherwise as a complete innings to be recorded as "Retired, Out."

BOWLED

LAW 34. The striker is out "Bowled"—If the wicket be bowled down, even if the ball first touch his bat or person.

OFFICIAL NOTES

1. The striker, after playing the ball, is out "Bowled" if he then kicks or hits it on to his wicket before the completion of his stroke.
2. The striker is out "Bowled" under this Law when the ball is deflected on to his wicket off his person, even though a decision against him might be justified under Law 39—L.B.W.

Additional Comment on Law 34.

The term "played on" is merely a descriptive one and should not be used in the score sheet.

CAUGHT

LAW 35. **The striker is out "Caught"—if the ball, from a stroke of the bat or of the hand holding the bat, but not the wrist, be held by a fieldsman before it touch the ground, although it be hugged to the body of the catcher, or be accidentally lodged in his dress. The fieldsman must have both his feet entirely within the playing area at the instant the catch is completed.**

Experiment:- *Since 1967 for all grades of cricket in the U.K., for the striker to be out "Caught", the Fieldsman must have no part of his body grounded outside the playing area in the act of making the catch and afterwards.*

OFFICIAL NOTES

1. Provided the ball does not touch the ground, the hand holding it may do so in effecting a catch.
2. The umpire is justified in disregarding the fact that the ball has touched the ground, or has been carried over the boundary provided that a catch has, in fact, been completed prior to such occurrence.

Experiment 1967. *The act of making the catch starts from the time when the Fieldsman first handles the ball.*

3. The fact that a ball has touched the striker's person before or after touching his bat does not invalidate a catch.
4. The striker may be "Caught" even if the fieldsman has not touched the ball with his hands, including the case of a ball lodging in the wicket-keeper's pads.
5. A fieldsman standing within the playing area may lean against the boundary to catch a ball, and this may be done even if the ball has passed over the boundary.
6. If the striker lawfully plays a ball a second time he may be out under this Law, but only if the ball has not touched the ground since being first struck.
7. The striker may be caught off any obstruction within the playing area provided it has not previously been decided on as a boundary.

"Caught"—see Note 5

"Out"—The hand may touch the ground provided the ball does not do so. See Law 35, Note 1

Additional Comments on Law 35.

A catch is regarded as "made" at the instant the fieldsman remaining in the field of play has complete control over the further disposal of the ball. The juggling of a catch ending in the ball being dropped may last a second or two, whereas the effective holding of a hot return may be instantaneous.

A special case of a "catch" not referred to in the official Notes is that of a ball hit back to the bowler who just touches it before it breaks the wicket at his end, with the non-striker out of his ground. If nothing further happens, on appeal the non-striker is out "Run out" but if the ball is caught by a fieldsman beyond the broken wicket without its having touched the ground at any time after being struck, the striker is out "Caught."

Note that the striker is not "caught" if a ball strikes a hand which is no longer holding the handle of the bat, *e.g.*, the striker may have taken a hand off to guard his face against a bouncer.

HANDLED THE BALL

LAW 36. Either batsman is out "Handled the ball"—If he touch it while in play with his hands, unless it be done at the request of the opposite side.

OFFICIAL NOTES

1. A hand holding the bat is regarded as part of it for the purposes of Laws 36, 37 and 39.
2. The correct entry in the score book when a batsman is given out under this Law is "Handled the Ball," and the bowler does not get credit for the wicket.

Additional Comments on Law 36.

The handling of the ball while it is in play by either batsman should never occur except at the specific request of the fielding side. If it does and there is an appeal, the umpires are bound by the Law to give the offender out.

The Law is not intended to apply to an involuntary handling such as a player protecting his face from a bouncer by taking his hand off the bat.

HIT THE BALL TWICE

LAW 37. The striker is out "Hit the ball twice"—

If the ball be struck or be stopped by any part of his person, and he wilfully strike it again, except for the sole purpose of guarding his wicket, which he may do with his bat or any part of his person, other than his hands. No runs except those which result from an overthrow shall be scored from a ball lawfully struck twice.

OFFICIAL NOTES

1. It is for the umpire to decide whether the ball has been so struck a second time legitimately or not. The umpire may regard the fact that a run is attempted as evidence of the batsmen's intention to take advantage of the second stroke, but it is not conclusive.
2. A batsman may not attempt to hit the ball twice, if in so doing he baulks the wicket-keeper or any fieldsman attempting to make a catch.
3. This Law is infringed if the striker, after playing the ball and without any request from the opposite side, uses his bat to return the ball to a fieldsman.
4. The correct entry in the score book when the striker is given out under this Law is "Hit the ball twice," and the bowler does not get credit for the wicket.

Additional Comment on Law 37.

Attention is specially drawn to Note 3—A batsman should not knock the ball back to the bowler, wicket-keeper or any fieldsman unless specifically asked to do so.

HIT WICKET

"Out"—Hit Wicket

LAW 38. The striker is out "Hit Wicket"—If in playing at the ball he hit down his wicket with his bat or any part of his person.

OFFICIAL NOTES

1. The striker is "Out" under this Law if:
   (i) In making a second stroke to keep the ball out of his wicket he hits it down.
   (ii) While playing at the ball, but not otherwise, his wicket is broken by his cap or hat falling, or by part of his bat.
2. A batsman is not out for breaking the wicket with his bat or person while in the act of running.

Experiment:- *In First Class cricket in the U.K. a batsman is out if he breaks the wicket in setting off for the first run.*

Additional Comments on Law 38.

The chief difficulty in applying this Law is to decide the end of the action of playing at the ball. Note 1 helps the solution of this point. The words should be interpreted to include any action of the striker's bat or person which occurs from the moment he starts to receive a delivery until the absolute conclusion of his attempt to play the ball—this includes for example the striker's swing round or follow through in playing a ball on the leg side. On the other hand the breaking of the wicket by the striker before the ball has left the bowler's hand could not normally contravene the Law.

If a striker is rendered unconscious by being struck and collapses on to the wicket this would not contravene the Law provided the umpire was satisfied that the wicket would not have been disturbed by the attempt to play the ball.

L.B.W.

LAW 39. The striker is out "Leg before wicket"—
If with any part of his person except his hand, which
is in a straight line between wicket and wicket, even
though the point of impact be above the level of
the bails, he intercept a ball which has not first
touched his bat or hand, and which, in the opinion
of the umpire, shall have, or would have, pitched
on a straight line from the bowler's wicket to the
striker's wicket, or shall have pitched on the off-
side of the striker's wicket, provided always that
the ball would have hit the wicket.

OFFICIAL NOTES

1. The word "hand" used in this Law should be interpreted as the hand holding the bat.
2. A batsman is only "Out" under this Law if *all* the four following questions are answered in the affirmative:
   (i) Would the ball have hit the wicket?
   (ii) Did the ball pitch on a straight line between wicket and wicket (and this case includes a ball intercepted full pitch by the striker), or did it pitch on the off-side of the striker's wicket?
   (iii) Was it part of the striker's person other than the hand which first intercepted the ball?
   (iv) Was that part of the striker's person in a straight line between wicket and wicket at the moment of impact, irrespective of the height of the point of impact?

Additional Comments on Law 39.

It is fundamental that the striker cannot be out L.B.W. from any ball pitched outside the line of the leg stump, or from one that would pass to either side or over the top of the wicket.

In connection with Law 39 the following are common misconceptions:—

(*a*) That the umpires must give the striker the benefit of any doubt.

(*b*) That bowlers who bowl round the wicket cannot ever succeed in appeals for L.B.W.

(*c*) That a striker who touches the ball with his bat before it strikes his person can be out L.B.W.

When a striker in playing forward is hit *full pitch* the umpire should be careful in deciding whether the ball would have hit the wicket or not: the chance of this may be small in the case of a ball which is swinging.

OBSTRUCTING THE FIELD

LAW 40. Either batsman is out "Obstructing the
field"—If he wilfully obstruct the opposite side;
should such wilful obstruction by either batsman
prevent a ball from being caught it is the striker
who is out.

OFFICIAL NOTES

1. The umpire must decide whether the obstruction was "wilful" or not. The involuntary interception by a batsman while running of a throw in is not in itself an offence.
2. The correct entry in the score book when a batsman is given out under this Law is "Obstructing the field," and the bowler does not get credit for the wicket.

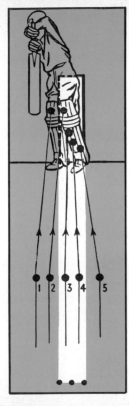

When a ball pitches between wicket and wicket, for a "L.B.W." appeal to be upheld, its later trajectory must be between the limits indicated by the dotted lines.

In the case of a ball pitching outside the line of the off stump the angle is narrower than in Example 1, since for an appeal for "L.B.W." to be justified the batsman must be hit on a part of his body between wicket and wicket.

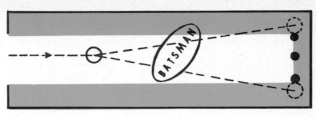

Example 1

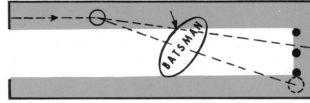

Example 2

Correct Decisions

Ball 1 — "Not Out" — point of impact — not between wicket and wicket.
Balls 2 and 3 — "Out," provided ball was not rising so as to pass over top of stumps.
Ball 4 — "Out" — Umpire must satisfy himself that the leg break is not so great as to cause ball to pass outside the off stump.
Ball 5 — "Not Out" — no ball pitching outside the line of the leg stump can justify a "L.B.W." decision.

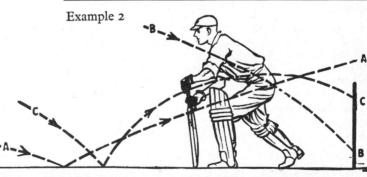

A   Ball lifting to pass over top of wicket—"Not Out".
B and C Ball dropping to hit wicket, the striker may be out in either case.

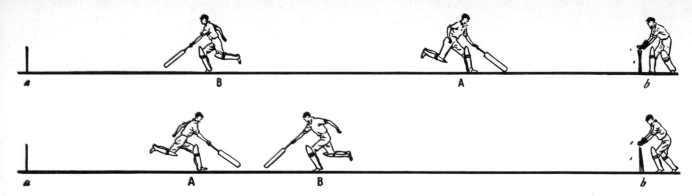

Top: Batsman A—"Run Out." Bottom: Batsman B—"Run Out."

RUN OUT

LAW 41. Either batsman is out "Run out"—If in running or at any time, while the ball is in play, he be out of his ground, and his wicket be put down by the opposite side. If the batsmen have crossed each other, he that runs for the wicket which is put down is out; if they have not crossed, he that has left the wicket which is put down is out. But unless he attempt to run, the striker shall not be given "Run out" in the circumstances stated in Law 42, even should "No Ball" have been called.

OFFICIAL NOTE

1. If the ball is played on to the opposite wicket, neither batsman is liable to be "Run out" unless the ball has been touched by a fieldsman before the wicket is put down.

Additional Comments on Law 41.

It is clear from Laws 41 and 42 that an appeal for "stumped" can only be justified if the wicket has been put down by the wicket-keeper without the ball being touched by any other fieldsman, and is limited by Law 42 to the actual time of the striker receiving the ball.

All other cases of appeals when a wicket is put down with a batsman out of his ground must come under Law 41, *i.e.*, "Run out."

The striker can never be stumped off a "No Ball" (see Law 42), nor can he be run out by the wicket-keeper without the intervention of some other fielder, unless he is attempting a run.

If a batsman remains in his ground and the other batsman joins him there, it is the latter who is run out if the farther wicket is put down.

STUMPED

LAW 42. The striker is out "Stumped"—If in receiving a ball, not being a "No Ball" delivered by the bowler, he be out of his ground otherwise than in attempting a run, and the wicket be put down by the wicket-keeper without the intervention of another fieldsman. Only when the ball has touched the bat or person of the striker may the wicket-keeper take it in front of the wicket for this purpose.

OFFICIAL NOTE

1. The striker may be "Stumped" if the wicket is broken by a ball rebounding from the wicket-keeper's person.

THE WICKET-KEEPER

LAW 43. The wicket-keeper shall remain wholly behind the wicket until a ball delivered by the bowler touches the bat or person of the striker, or passes the wicket, or until the striker attempts a run. Should the wicket-keeper contravene this Law, the striker shall not be out except under Laws 36, 37, 40 and 41 and then only subject to Law 46.

OFFICIAL NOTES

1. This Law is provided to secure to the striker his right to play the ball and to guard his wicket without interference from the wicket-keeper. The striker may not be penalised if in the legitimate defence of his wicket he interferes with the wicket-keeper, except as provided for in Law 37. Note 2.

2. If, in the opinion of the umpire, the encroachment by the wicket-keeper has not gained any advantage for the fielding side, nor in any way has interfered with the right of the striker to play the ball with complete freedom, nor has had any effect whatsoever on the dismissal of the striker, he shall disregard the infringement.

Additional Comments on Law 42.

Law 42 clearly states when the wicket-keeper may take the ball in front of the wicket. In the sketch the wicket-keeper has taken the ball in front of the wicket, and if the ball has not been touched, he cannot put down the wicket in order to stump the striker.

The wicket-keeper if standing back, can throw the ball at the wicket, or put it down in any of the ways provided in Law 31. Under Note 1 a ball rebounding off the wicket-keeper's pads (or kicked by him on to the wicket) also justifies an appeal for stumping.

Ball taken in front of wicket. "Not out" unless the striker has played the ball.

THE FIELDSMAN

LAW 44. The fieldsman may stop the ball with any part of his person, but if he wilfully stop it otherwise, 5 runs shall be added to the run or runs already made; if no run has been made 5 shall be scored. The penalty shall be added to the score of the striker if the ball has been struck, but otherwise to the score of byes, leg byes, no balls or wides as the case may be.

OFFICIAL NOTES

1. A fieldsman must not use his cap, etc., for the purpose of fielding a ball.
2. The 5 runs are a penalty and the batsmen do not change ends.

Experiment:- *Since 1967 for all grades of cricket in the U.K., the number of on-side Fielders behind the popping crease at the instant of the Bowler's delivery shall not exceed two. In some other countries the number of on-side Fieldsmen is limited to 5. For infringement the Umpire calls "No Ball".*

DUTIES OF THE UMPIRES

LAW 45. Before the toss for innings, the umpires shall acquaint themselves with any special regulations, and shall agree with both captains on any other conditions affecting the conduct of the match; shall satisfy themselves that the wickets are properly pitched; and shall agree between themselves on the watch or clock to be followed during play.

OFFICIAL NOTES

1. Apart from "Special Regulations" (see Law 10, Note 1), other conditions of play within the framework of the Laws are frequently necessary, e.g., Hours of play, Intervals, etc.
2. The captains are entitled to know which clock or watch will be followed during play.

Comparing watches

Additional Comment on Law 45.

If in a one or half-day match the innings are restricted by time or a specified number of overs, it is essential that the umpires should ensure that both captains are clear as to the agreed conditions.

LAW 46. Before and during a match the umpires shall ensure that the conduct of the game and the implements used are strictly in accordance with the Laws; they are the sole judges of fair and unfair play, and the final judges of the fitness of the ground, the weather and the light for play in the event of the decision being left to them; all disputes shall be determined by them, and if they disagree the actual state of things shall continue. The umpires shall change ends after each side has had one innings.

OFFICIAL NOTES

1. An umpire should stand where he can best see any act upon which his decision may be required. Subject to this over-riding consideration the umpire at the bowler's end should stand where he does not interfere with either the bowler's run up or the striker's view. If the other umpire wishes to stand on the off instead of the leg side of the pitch, he should obtain the permission of the captain of the fielding side and inform the batsman.

2. The umpires must not allow the attitude of the players or spectators to influence their decisions under the Laws.

3. A code of signals for umpires is laid down in the Notes to the relevant Laws; but an umpire must call as well as signal, if necessary, to inform the players and scorers.

4. FAIR AND UNFAIR PLAY

    (i) The umpires are entitled to intervene without appeal in the case of unfair play, but should not otherwise interfere with the progress of the game, except as required to do so by the Laws.

    (ii) In the event of a player failing to comply with the instructions of an umpire or criticising his decisions, the umpires should in the first place request the captains to take action, and if this proves ineffective, report the incident forthwith to the executives of the teams taking part in the match.

    (iii) It is illegal for a player to lift the seam of the ball in order to obtain a better hold. In such a case the umpire will, if necessary, change the ball for one which has had similar wear, and will warn the captain that the practice is unfair. The use of resin, wax, etc., by bowlers is also unfair, but a bowler may dry the ball when wet on a towel or with sawdust.

Experiment:- *The bowler only shall be allowed to polish the ball.*

    (iv) An umpire is justified in intervening under this Law should any player of the fielding side incommode the striker by any noise or motion while he is receiving a ball.

    (v) It is the duty of the umpires to intervene and prevent players from causing damage to the pitch which may assist the bowlers.

    (vi) The persistent bowling of fast, short-pitched balls at the batsman is unfair if, in the opinion of the umpire at the bowler's end, it constitutes a systematic attempt at intimidation. In such event he must adopt the following procedure:

    (a) When he decides that such bowling is becoming persistent he forthwith "cautions" the bowler.

    (b) If this "caution" is ineffective, he informs the captain of the fielding side and the other umpire of what has occurred. (*continued overleaf*)

(c) Should the above prove ineffective, the umpire at the bowler's end must:

    (i) At the first repetition call "Dead Ball," when the over is regarded as completed.

(ii) Direct the captain of the fielding side to take the bowler off forthwith. The captain shall take the bowler off as directed.

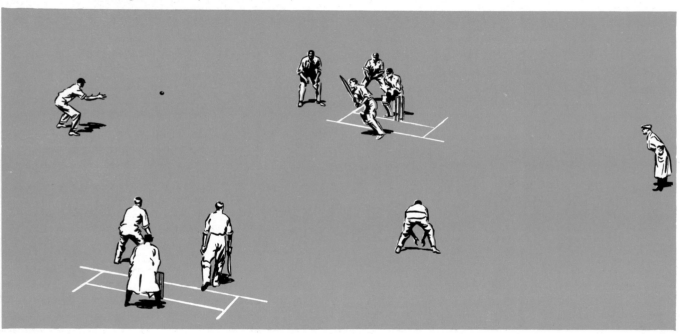

Position of Umpires—see Law 46

(iii) Report the occurrence to the captain of the batting side as soon as an interval of play takes place.

A bowler who has been "taken off" as above may not bowl again during the same innings.

(vii) Any attempt by the batsmen to *steal a run* during the bowler's run up is unfair. Unless the bowler throws the ball at either wicket (see Laws 26, Note 3 and 27, Note 2), the umpire should call "Dead Ball" as soon as the batsmen cross in any such attempt to run, after which they return to their original wickets.

(viii) No player shall leave the field for the purpose of having a rub down or shower while play is actually in progress.

5. GROUND, WEATHER AND LIGHT

(i) Unless agreement to the contrary is made before the start of a match, the captains (during actual play the batsmen at the wickets may deputise for their captain) may elect to decide in regard to the fitness of the ground, weather, or light for play; otherwise, or in the event of disagreement, the umpires are required to decide.

(ii) Play should only be suspended when the conditions are so bad that it is unreasonable or dangerous for it to continue. The ground is unfit for play when water stands on the surface or when it is so wet or slippery as to deprive the batsmen or bowlers of a reasonable foothold, or the fieldsmen of the power of free movement. Play should *not* be suspended merely because the grass is wet and the ball slippery.

(iii) After any suspension of play, the captains, or, if the decision has been left to them, the umpires, unaccompanied by any of the players, will without further instruction carry out an inspection immediately the conditions improve, and will continue to inspect at intervals. Immediately the responsible parties decide that play is possible, they must call upon the players to resume the game.

Additional Comments on Law 46.

With reference to Note 1 it is clearly in the interest of the fielding side that the umpire's view should be unobstructed. They will therefore seldom be wise to press the umpire to stand where he does not want to; they can never insist on his doing so.

An umpire is not required to inform an incoming batsman of the number of balls remaining in the "Over" in progress, but he should give the information if asked for it. An umpire should not call "Last Over" before any interval or close of play.

In a one-day match the umpires do not change ends before each side has completed an innings.

With reference to Note 4, while the wearing of gloves by the wicket-keeper is an understood practice, fieldsmen should not wear gloves, bandages, or plaster to protect their hands, without the consent of the opposing captain, and then only if special circumstances necessitate it. The umpires should enquire if permission has been granted in such cases.

With reference to Note 5, it should be noted that the play should only be suspended if conditions are so bad that it is dangerous or unreasonable to continue.

APPEALS

LAW 47. The umpires shall not order a batsman out unless appealed to by the other side which shall be done prior to the delivery of the next ball, and before "Time" is called under Law 18. The umpire at the bowler's wicket shall answer appeals before the other umpire in all cases except those arising out of Laws 38 or 42, and out of Law 41 for run out at the striker's wicket. In any case in which an umpire is unable to give a decision, he shall appeal to the other umpire whose decision shall be final.

OFFICIAL NOTES

1. An appeal, "How's that?" covers all ways of being out (within the jurisdiction of the umpire appealed to), unless a specific way of getting out is stated by the person asking. When either umpire has given a batsman "Not out" the other umpire may answer any appeal within his jurisdiction, provided it is made in time.

2. The umpire signals "Out" by raising the index finger above the head. If the batsman is not out, the umpire calls "Not out."

3. An umpire may alter his decision provided that such alteration is made promptly.

4. Nothing in this Law prevents an umpire before giving a decision from consulting the other umpire on a point of fact which the latter may have been in a better position to observe. An umpire should not appeal to the other umpire in cases on which he could give a decision, merely because he is unwilling to give that decision. If after consultation, he is still in any doubt, the principle laid down in Law 46 applies and the decision will be in favour of the batsman.

5. The umpires should intervene if satisfied that a batsman, not having been given out, has left his wicket under a misapprehension.

6. Under Law 25 the ball is "Dead" on "Over" being called; this does not invalidate an appeal made prior to the first ball of the following "Over", provided the bails have not been removed by both umpires after "Time" has been called.

Additional Comments on Law 47.

By custom in many cases where the decision is obvious, no appeal is made and the batsmen accept their dismissal.

If an unjustified appeal is made for say L.B.W. and the striker is out caught or bowled, the umpire is fully justified in dealing with the appeal.

If an appeal is delayed, and runs are made before a batsman is given out, the umpires should instruct the scorers to disregard any runs to which the batting side are not entitled, e.g., if before the striker is given out L.B.W. the batsmen have run a "Leg Bye," this run should be disallowed and the non-striker should return to his original end.

Note 5, of course, does not protect a batsman who leaves his ground while the ball is in play, e.g., a batsman wrongly expecting a catch to be caught, leaves his ground and as a result is "Run Out."

UMPIRE'S SIGNALS

"Out"

"Leg Bye"

"Bye"

"Wide"

"No Ball"

"One Short"

"Boundary 4"

"Boundary 6"

1. (a) Law 4 explains the status of the scorers in relation to the umpires.

   (b) During the progress of the game, if two scorers have been appointed, they should frequently check the total to ensure that the score sheets agree.

   (c) The following method of entering "No Balls" and "Wides" (Laws 27 and 29) in the score sheet is recommended:

   (i) If no run is scored from the bat off a "No Ball" the latter should be entered as an "Extra," and a dot placed in the bowling analysis with a circle round it to show that the ball does not count in the over.

   (ii) If runs are scored from the bat off a "No Ball", they should be credited to the striker, and entered in the bowling analysis with a circle round the figure. Such runs count against the bowler in his analysis even though the ball does not count in the over.

   (iii) All runs scored from "Wide Balls" are entered as "Extras," and inserted in the bowler's analysis with a cross to indicate that the ball does not count in the over.

2. The following code of signalling between the umpires and the scorers has been approved:
   Boundaries—by waving the hand from side to side.
   A boundary six—by raising both arms above the head.
   Byes—by raising the open hand above the head.
   Leg Byes—by touching a raised knee with the hand.
   Wides—by extending both arms horizontally.
   No Balls—by extending one arm horizontally.
   The decision "Out"—by raising the index finger above the head.

   "One Short"—by bending the arm upwards and by touching the top of the nearest shoulder with the tips of the fingers of one hand.

3. If the above instructions are properly carried out, cases of disagreement as regards the scores and the results of matches should not occur.

It is, however, important that the captains should satisfy themselves of the correctness of the scores on the conclusion of play, as errors cannot subsequently be corrected.

It should be noted that, in general, by accepting the result notified by the scorers, the captain of the losing side has thereby acquiesced in the "playing out or giving up" of the match as stated in Law 22.

Additional Notes for Scorers.

1. The chief responsibility of the scorers is to ensure that at the conclusion of a match no doubts can be raised in regard to the accuracy of the score, and particularly so when the scores are almost the same. The scorers should agree on the details of the score on the fall of each wicket, and more often if necessary.

Law 4 does not lay down the number of scorers, but in a match of any importance there should always be one for each side, in addition to any assistants responsible for altering the telegraph.

If there is only one scorer, his responsibility for the absolute accuracy of the score is naturally all the greater.

Under Law 4, and Note 1 thereto, scorers have no authority to interfere with the game but they may consult the umpires at any time, and they should always do so at once if any doubt exists which affects the aggregate score.

Apart from being meticulously accurate, scorers should always take a pride in the neatness of their work, and provide themselves with well-sharpened pencils, and a clean india-rubber.

2. An example of a well-compiled score sheet for an innings, including the bowlers' analyses, will be found on pages 46 and 47.

When the final analysis of each bowler has been extracted, the total of runs, of "No Balls" and of "Wides" should each be the same as those shown in the main body of the score sheet, but "Byes" and "Leg Byes" in the latter do not appear anywhere in the bowlers' analyses.

3. Scorers must carefully note the provisions of Law 19 as regards the scoring of runs, when "One Short" has been called, or when a batsman is run out or caught.

4. The main points of difficulty for scorers arise in connection with the entry of "No Balls" and "Wides" in the analysis, to ensure that the cross check mentioned in paragraph 2 is possible.

(i) "No Balls" which are *not played* by the striker and all "Wides" are dealt with similarly. If the batsmen do not run at all, or take only 1 run, 1 "No Ball" or 1 "Wide" are entered both as Extras in the score, and in the bowling analysis.

If more than 1 run is taken, or the ball goes to the boundary, all such runs are similarly entered as "No Balls' or "Wides."

The conventional entries in such cases are:
⊙ for 1 "No Ball" or ✛ for 1 "Wide,"
☺ for 3 "No Balls" or ✢ for 4 "Wides."

(ii) "No Balls" which the striker *plays* are entered as follows:—

No run taken—as in (i) above.

One or more runs taken—credited to the striker and entered against bowler as "Runs" and *not* as "No Balls" under Extras.

The conventional entry in such cases is:
① for a single run or
③ for 3 runs.

(iii) The penalty of 1 for both a "No Ball" and a "Wide" is never credited *in addition* to runs or boundary allowances.

The penalty *still applies* even if a batsman is out off a "No Ball" (he can be "run out" or out for handling the ball, for hitting the ball twice or for obstructing the field), or off a "Wide" (he can be "run out" or stumped or out for handling the ball, hitting his wicket, or for obstructing the field).

Since the bowler can only get credit for the striker hitting his wicket, or for a stumping, the analysis entry in all other cases is as indicated in paragraph 4 (i) and (ii)—in the two cases in which the bowler, after bowling a "Wide," does get credit the conventional entry is ✛W indicating that the penalty applies even though the wicket is credited.

This point is of special interest when the last wicket is taken off a "No Ball" or "Wide" when the scores are level.

5. The scoring conventions connected with "Maiden" overs are of less importance.

A "Maiden" over is one in which no runs off the bat are scored, and by custom scorers do not regard the bowling of a "No Ball" (unless runs are scored off it) or a "Wide" as cancelling a "Maiden". (See illustration—1st over bowled by Bailey, page 47.)

At the end of a "Maiden" over—the dots in the analysis are joined together to form the letter "M"—if a wicket falls during a "Maiden" over some scorers join the dots to form the letter "W."

2nd INNINGS OF Regent Boys Club

ORDER OF GOING IN	BATSMAN'S NAME	SCORE	HOW OUT	BOWLER'S NAME	TOTAL RUNS
1	A. G. Hill	1 2 1 3 1 4 3 1 1 /	S^ca^ Roberts	O'Brien	1 7
2	P. W. Wilson	3 1 1 1 4 1 1 3 1 3 4 1 1 2 1 /	S^ca^ Roberts	O'Brien	2 8
3	G. Storer	1 4 1 /	S^ca^ Roberts	O'Brien	6
4	W. B. Turner	1 /	Bowled	Robinson	1
5	L. Ashby	0 2 1 2 1 3 2 1 1 1 1 1 1 2 1 4 1 3 1 1 4 3 1 2 2	Not	Out	4 5
6	D. A. Taylor	1 1 /	L. B. W	O'Brien	2
7	R. Newman	1 2 1 1 1 2 /	Bowled	Bailey	8
8	T. W. Martin	/	Bowled	Bailey	0
9	G. H. Hill	/	C^t^ Morton	O'Brien	0
10	M. Clarke	/	Bowled	Bailey	0
11	L. M. Smith		Absent		-

BYES 3 1 2   LEG BYES   WIDE BALLS 1 1   NO BALLS   8

RUNS AT THE FALL OF EACH WICKET	1 FOR 33	2 FOR 45	3 FOR 50	4 FOR 72	5 FOR 84	6 FOR 108	7 FOR 108	8 FOR 111	9 FOR 115	10 FOR	TOTAL	1 1 5

Typical Score Sheet

BOWLERS' NAMES	WIDES	NO BALLS	NUMBER OF OVERS AND RUNS MADE FROM EACH BOWLER								TOTALS					
			(1–20 over-by-over markings)								OVERS	MAIDENS	RUNS	WIDES	NO BALLS	WICKETS
J. S. Bailey											9·2	3	21	2	–	3
G. Watts											5	1	7	–	–	–
S. O'Brien											21	5	59	–	–	5
Robinson											16	7	20			1

Typical Bowling Analysis

INDEX